Please return/renew this item by the last date shown.

North
Somerset
C O U N C I L

D0233505

PRAISES

Elizabeth Jennings

Praises

CARCANET

for Catherine Jones

First published in 1998 by
Carcanet Press Limited
4th Floor, Conavon Court
12-16 Blackfriars Street
Manchester M3 5BQ

A CIP catalogue record for this book
is available from the British Library
ISBN 1 85754 399 8

The publisher acknowledges financial assistance
from the Arts Council of England

Set in 10pt Palatino by Bryan Williamson, Frome
Printed and bound in England by SRP Ltd, Exeter

Contents

6

For my Sister, now a Widow

Mourners have tip-toed away, the flowers are dead.
A mocking winter sun pours through the glass
Of your bedroom windows, but your grief won't pass.
Slowly, carefully you make the marriage-bed.

I think of you crying alone and cannot bear
The thought of it long. What can I do to make
Each day more kindly? Maybe though for his sake
You want to keep his loss, for he is there,

There in the harsh reminder of these things,
Mostly little ones certainly such as
The way he washed up the breakfast, hoovered the floor.
Are you cross with a happy bird which sings

Close to the house? No, I don't think so.
There's never been anything morbid or selfish about
The world you've managed. Still it has to go
On working without solace or a doubt.

I've been surprised into a new compassion.
Of course I've known it in different guises before
But not like this which feels like a fraught passion.
It makes me hope there'll be many rings at your door.

It arose when I saw you look so pale and dressed
Not in black but muted colours. I want to say,
You have nothing to blame yourself for. Whenever you pray
I feel sure that, even so, you have confessed

To little impatiences, words out of place.
Listen to me: your husband loved you so
That, like a lover, he always looked at you,
You were his reason to live, his channel of grace.

A View of Lazarus

See he is coming from the tomb. His eyes
Need shelter from the light. We crowd and press
Towards him, some say nothing. One or two
Whisper. Others look afraid but stare,
Most turn their eyes away. Such a strange
Light is coming from behind the man
Brought back from death and coughing in the breeze.
One by one his senses set to work
To ease this man to us. A look of loss
Shows on his features but he does not speak.
Some begin to question him about
What dying felt like and how did he break
Back to us. He can relieve our doubt,
But he seems dumb and we don't want to make
His rising difficult although we long
To look back at the glimmering Kingdom he
Has left, if Paradise is there
But is not for the snatching. Lazarus now
Opens his eyes and it's at us he stares
As if we all were strangers. Then it's odd,
But we feel we should stop talking. Lazarus is,
Yes no doubt of it, now shedding tears,
And whispering quietly, God, O no, dear God.

Walking in the Dark

In a dark mood I wandered at night-time,
Most people were in bed, some lights still shone.
In the far distance; trains made happy sounds,
A going off with jubilation. I
      Tried to think of them,
      In childhood distant trains
      Were a good lullaby.
But now I was grown-up and wandered looking . . . for what . . . ?
I did not know and yet I felt my spirit
Stirring with some glad power.
Between a dream and a nightmare I had come
To this strange city not on any map
That I'd been shown at school
And yet I knew I had to take quiet steps
Even as I felt afraid of crossing
Almost every street. What fear was this?
Where did it come from? Why
Had it made me think
I must put on a jacket and go out?
The season was so vague, the moon was half
But not a star was there for me to look at,
Not a human-being anywhere
Could join this search whose goal I did not know.
The God whom I had always prayed to still
Existed but he seemed too far away
To give a blessing or explain why I
Had to walk upon what was perhaps
A pilgrimage though there was not a sign
In air, on ground, close to the moon, to say
I must know dark and carry it about.
Dear God, this was a doubt about a doubt.

In and Out of Time

He has heralded the morning with his blessing.
　　The Great Christ has done this
Not 'done' but 'does' for past is always missing
When Jesus comes in all his mysteries.

Time is our worry and our pain. We must
　　Be shackled to it till
We have done penance for our pride and lust
And all the deadly sins which tease our will.

Clocks chime, bells ring. The present slips away
　　Even as we make
The good choice or the bad. We know of day
Even as the Precious Blood we take,

And eat the Bread, for these are lasting things,
　　And Heaven's gate's ajar
As in humbleness our spirit sings
And we learn galaxies, name every star.

Cheap gibes are made about a God who can
　　Allow us to feel pain.
But we learn sympathy for God-made-Man
And touch eternal things again, again.

The Words are Pouring

The words are pouring. Listen to their sound,
Their implication, weather, strength and cry,
Let dictionaries shout against the wind
And lyricism find its weather there.
Here's a world of freedom hardly won,
The fervent sun is beating on our faces,
Grace is found, religions praise themselves
And men stand back as if creation's day
Were now and here, and all attempt to pray.

The weather of the world is altering.
Babel begins again, the many tongues
Of fraught mankind are fighting as they sing,
When once more can that younger John be heard –
'In the beginning always is the Word'?

Rapture of Spring

Play havoc with our language. It is Spring.
Let nouns be adjectives and every adjective
Become an adverb. Let the language sing
As daffodils blow trumpets and the life
Of every bird takes wing.

The sap is running and the rainbow is
Pouring its colours out while every sense
Vies with the others in a wreath of praise,
A purpose of pure joy. Sweet innocence
Marches through our days.

Always something new is found to say.
We are so glad, our blood is sap also,
We speak in joy at all this ripe display
And point up to the sun with work to do.
O see, it too can pray.

A Unique Gift

Don't be embarrassed by the words I write.
    You should know they are true.
To you I owe the kindness of tonight
    And its wide peace also.

I have been angry, difficult at times
    And shall be yet again.
But there is peace in these warm, Summer rhymes.
    You've helped me to attain

A place and mood of hope. Desire alone
    Cannot accomplish this,
Much work is needed and much care. You own
    A gift that few possess.

Somehow you know how to make magic happen.
It's here before me with the curtains open.

An Apple Tree

The apple tree, so many kinds
And there's the one which few forget,
But I'm concerned with one which finds
Rich sun and I am near to it.
As I draw blinds
Against this sudden August heat
I think of one who lived and died
Where I have come. So soon we'll eat
All apple harvests. Polished, dried
Apples may be sweet
Or tart, or juicy. Of the lot
The Cox's Orange is the one
I like the best,
That special sweetness of its own.
I wonder what

The lady who lived here liked best.
A friend talked of her with much love
And said the apple-tree brought rest
To her. She wrote a poem as proof
This tree was specially graced.
What a happy change it is
That someone saw the better side
Of ill-fabled apple trees.
We're taught the reason why man died
To trust was eating this

One fruit, and now in all of us
Bad choices often rule our world,
Bringing famished hate, abuse,
But my forerunner who was old
Hymned the apple-tree across
The way. Her writing made it gold.
Her dying must have wrought much loss
(I know that's true, I have been told)
But still her apple tree stands bold
And I am lucky to live where
It flaunts its foliage in green air.

A Full Moon

Tonight the full moon is the Host held up
    For everybody's eyes
To see and understand the high and deep
    Salvation in the skies.
In usual Masses we withdraw our stares
When we bow down. How wise

The Godhead is to make all Masses small,
    All Consecrations set
Where the most simple, the most sceptical
    Know of mankind's regret
That we brought Christ himself to such a pass.
    That overflowing grace

Gave us another chance when we refused
    To leave one Tree alone.
God-became-Man because of this and used
    A cruel cross to atone
For us. It seems we cannot bear for long
A simple goodness but must choose the wrong

Because it looks so sweet. But look again
    That Host-like moon shines where
All can see him. Christ took on all pain
    Beyond time's arbiter.
The Bread is offered us, the wine also
For Christ and every saint, his Mother too.
    That moon in silence can
Elevate us till we long to know
    The Trinity's whole plan.
Nature was fashioned for this purpose. See
A moon reminds us of God's ministry.

Song Just Before Autumn

It is a music of the air,
    It is a spell that's cast around
The trees. Here is the harbinger
    Of Autumn. On the ground

Gold's tossed and squandered. Never mind,
    The breezes haunt and hunt. Each star
Is diamond-fixed. We soon shall find
    That almost-Winter's here

But not quite yet. There's time and space
    For worthy fallings, songs and things
That have no words except pure grace
    And all its whisperings.

Harvest Home

The music of Autumn is just on the edge of hearing,
The torches of Autumn glance to and fro in the trees,
The still-green trees, not a shadow showing among them
The smells of Autumn are noticed when the winds
Of Summer's lightness slow. The soil is rich, the corn has been
    brought in,
Soon the blackberries with their dark, jewel shapes
Will hang and ask to be picked.
The signs and tokens, the myths, the Natural History
Of Autumn are never like last year's or the next.
Weather is unexpected. A shrewd guess
Is as good as a meteorology of measures.
Listen, feel, sniff. What do you hear, and what do you taste?
A library of intentions, a churchful of bygone prayers

But – and this is the best of all –
A Harvest Home of a Brass Band shining and blowing,
Reaching the heart-beats and going far beyond them.
Everything Golden with Brass. It is mid-September
And watching and listening to this marching of Bands
I feel the world is celebrating itself.
Heedless, almost, of our presences altogether,
But our spirits enter the instruments that are blown,
Crash with the big cymbals and meet each other
Never mind that Winter is round the corner,
With music and touching and smelling the news of our world.
We are ripe for whatever comes.

Alone Over Christmas

A serious night of calm it is. The moon
More than half. How warm it is for Winter.
Christmas will be on us very soon.
It is the time of Advent Calendars
       And I sit down alone

Happy and full of friendship but I think
Of a young man who at the weekend stood
Calling 'Everyone's walking past.' Some brink
Of lonely terror was near him. It's no good
       Pretending every link

Between each human being and another
At Christmas suddenly grows firm and solid.
This lonely man is everybody's brother
And we *do* walk past in selfish mood
       Not bothering to bother.

No Visions or Prayers

I am not after visions or prayers
Nor in search of experience missed in earlier days.
Least of all do I carry a message, invoke a cause or yield my
    sympathy.
I am not even sure yet what it is that I am pursuing
But the feel of something just out of reach of my writing,
Beyond the luck which is almost half of each poem.
No word is on the tip of my mind or hidden
Waiting for me to find it.

I am only partly aware of the plan, the music, the theme
Yet I feel that some time I shall come upon it.
It may be narrow or wide
It may be a tone in music
It may be – and now I think I am getting nearer –
A flow of song, a cadence that hints and surprises
That carries me into maybe a darkness of the spirit –
That has to be risked –
But I am eager and ardent, baffled and angry.
Two nights ago a thread of sound came near sleep.
The subject is totally hidden
But a whisper, a hand, an accidental leader
Drove me, O, to such pure and utterly new
Story or passion. Something is plucking a string
And feels like a lover's first touch.

Apology to a Friend
(for C.J.)

People say 'You're sensitive.' I'm not.
        Only an hour ago
Unwittingly I hurt someone when what
I feel for them is rich and ought to grow.

Why did I not think hard of what I said
        And learn that possibly
You felt quite differently about one dead,
A young and public figure? I could be

So cool, no, worse, so cold and be like ice
        About this unknown one.
Too late, I saw the sadness in your eyes.
What have I done today, and what undone?

Round and Round

The children asked 'Where is the end of the world?'
And we started telling them about horizons
And how the sun does not really go down
As it seems to us to be doing.

They were all frowning and obviously didn't believe us.
We looked at each other and wordlessly agreed
That scientific speeches were useless and so
After a fairly long pause
We told them all the ancient stories
About the sun moving around the world
And rising and setting over and over again.
They listened, did not speak, but they stopped frowning
When we said, 'Of course that isn't quite true',
They put their hands over their ears and ran out
Letting what we call knowledge lag behind them.

Famous Parents

'Are you his daughter?' Don't you feel a blank,
Like someone overlooked and in the way
Because you are a relative? You thank
For being attached to this great man, don't say
But surely think 'I am myself.' You may

Give well-worn smiles, 'Oh yes my father was
A sweet and generous man.' He was a swine,
Had filthy habits. And you, just because
You are his child must sometimes want to whine
'I hated him. Nothing was ever mine.'

But then a famous father or a mother
May well have been adorable and gave
You love and wit and money. You'd still bother
About taking advantage of a love
So overblown. Still you'd want to move

Away and change your name. For you're not 'Me'
As ordinary, lucky people are.
Your father gave you fame lopsidedly.
'I am myself,' you cry, 'and not a star.'
These famous by their birth will not go far.
Wiser not to try. Forget me, *He*.

Childhood Christmas Parties

Those parties after Christmas always threw
     A shadow back upon
The joyous gifts, events, so much to do
And all things glittering. But there was no sun

To light the parties we had to attend.
     Children are stoical, don't say
'I do not want to go.' They go and bend
To order. How I hated all those games.
     I never found a chair
When the music ended. All bad dreams
I'd known came true and yet I would stand there

Trying to smile, begging God to make
     Six o'clock less slow
To come, but when it struck a smile would break
Out. Most thought I did not want to go.

Ballad of a Thinker

One man went out and watched the sun
And found it warm and stayed beneath
Its casual power. 'Much can be done,'
He thought, 'when there's warm air to breathe

And heat just right, not tropical.'
He sat down to his work and did
Not note the time. His mind was full
Of words and concepts. Each one led

To others and his argument
Was sweet to read. He called out to
A woman who appeared. She leant
Upon his shoulder. She went through

His reasoning and her eyes shone,
'Life will be easier now,' she said.
'A kind of magic you have done.
I feel it ringing round my head.'

So he went on with happy ease,
With confidence supplied by her.
He'd found a world made just to please
Because a valid truth was there.

The sun was strong. The air was wide.
The plan and purpose pleased this man.
He never thought that he should hide
From fiery heat. The hours began

To slow and every thought was laid
Upon a page. The man lay there
But suddenly some difference made
Him stir. He woke and wept for where

His pleasant arguments were set
Upon his note-book there was now
Only an empty page. He let
The pages flutter, wondered how

He'd tell the woman of the change,
But she had gone. She was a part
Of his deep dream. He must arrange
His life again. He had to start

Upon his own, the sun gone cold.
'I want my dream,' he cried, but knew
Dreams won't revive however bold
The dreamer is. That this is true

Is how the actual brings us down
And scatters magic quite away.
'When I'm awake and quite alone
The world's not mine and will not stay.'

Teenagers

Adolescence seems less painful now
    Than it was when I too
Found I had changed. Few would then allow
For all the questioning I had to do.

Soon it was a questioning of thought
    And of Faith and self.
All I had once accepted was in doubt.
I was half a child and also – half –

A grown-up person. Nothing fitted me,
    The world seemed made for all
The eager walkers, talkers, wholly free.
I was clumsy, awkward, letting fall

Almost everything I touched. I could
    Not take one thing on trust.
I tried to change each dark and doubting mood.
Simply to hide was what I wanted most.

It is very likely that beneath the smart
    Looks and words, among
These, teenagers hide what there's no art
To mend. I mean the pangs of being young.

Boston

I've never been back to Boston,
Boston, Lincolnshire,
Never looked at the Stump with grown-up eyes,
Never stepped on the flat ground or seen the size
Of the sky unencumbered by hills or trees.
All I remember is

Being pushed in a pram after an illness, playing
On a Pogo-stick (one plaything that's never returned),
I remember cutting the garden hedge with scissors
And picking the red and black currants and gooseberries.
I remember the nursery table where we used to play Ludo,
Once I lost and picked up the board and threw down the pieces
And can't remember if I was chided for this.

So often people say, 'You don't remember things and
All these memories, all these scenes and emotions.'
But they're wrong. My senses tingle when I think of
The smell of bonfires, touch of nettles and
A season wrapped in what five senses tell.

But I sometimes long for a music of memory
A song with a rhythm, and blackbirds singing high,
For the ear is swiftly attuned to happiness.
It's on the edge of my mind but always stays there
As the hint of a note, a recalcitrant, teasing sound
Which ears can't catch and push it into my mind.
In fact if I think of birdsong it's never connected
With Boston, Lincolnshire.
But what my ears lack is richly made up with scenes,
The white, cool dress of my Nanny in the moonlight
And the moon in several shapes staring at me
Surrounded by a majesty of stars
And sky was heaven and God the Father lived
Beyond the moon, beyond the stars, up there
High above everything, keeping order where
I once stared up in Boston, Lincolnshire.

Theatre

Theatre of the Absurd, Theatre of Cruelty, Theatre
Of the here and now, the actual, the spare
Moments of revelation, then the bleak
Look at meetings and departures showing
All lack of understanding, people never
Able to touch or extend or assist each other.
Then there's the Theatre of Ideas and wit
Based on a casual meeting or stray acquaintance.

But why not the bold and brash, the hurting and
The broken heart needing putting together?
Why not the real endeavours, the warmth withheld
Then wasted in a cruel act regretted
Almost as if it hadn't truly happened?
Why are we niggardly? Why not fuller, willing
To forget or lose each other or lead back?
I cannot say and yet I fight to drive off

The theatre Shakespeare spread across our land
And down our history, and all Europe's stance.
Who will be bold, who dare take the risk
Of ending a fool when there's any chance
Of a rich loving or a tender tryst?
The curtains rise and fall on littlenesses,
The great surrenders happen in the wings.

Praises

I praise those things I always take for granted:–
The tap my sister turns on for my bath
Every time I stay, the safety pin –
And who invented it? I do not know –
The comb, the piece of soap, a shoe, its shine,
The name tape and the string, a leather purse –
How they all flock as I recall them now,
And Now I also praise with all it holds
Of nudges, hand-shakes, playing trains with children.
There is no end until I'm tired and think
Of craftsmen everywhere . . . O I forgot,
Cushions, napkins, stoves and cubes of ice.
All the world is praise or else is war.
Tonight the moon is almost half in shape,
'Tomorrow will be hot' say weathermen.
I praise the yawning kind of sleep that's coming,
And where the spirit goes, the sheet, the pillow . . .

Reasons for Not Returning

I

They say 'Go back to it.' They mean to Rome
Where I was happy forty years ago.
All was excitement. I had not left home
For such a time before. There I could grow

Into a different person in some ways
And those important. I walked with a map
And guide-book daily, everywhere would gaze
And then I fell into the generous lap

Of History and Faith. The latter I
Shared, though English, I was glad I knew
French and Latin. They helped me to try

The language; when I did, people would show
Delight and say 'Bravo'. Until I die
I'll keep my Rome. I never want to go

II

Back because all foreign places are
Bursting with tourists now. Cities you love
Are more than stone and brick. You travel far
And find a mood, a purpose. I won't move

A step to go back to the Rome in which
I learnt how time and history compete.
Almost every street in Rome is rich
With fountains, pictures and good meals to eat.

I sometimes close my eyes and swiftly see
Every street and statue, every large
And little church. I met new friends who'd be

In my life always. Such a privilege
Rome was in every vital way to me,
Now she's a state of mind in my old age.

Carol for 1997

Made flesh, made poetry, made art,
    The little child was born for this.
His mother held him to her heart
    And touched his brow with her warm kiss,
    Underneath a bursting star
    This God-Child came to us from far.

And every Christmas once again
    He's born afresh and needs our care.
He is all hope yet knows of pain
    For on a cross he'll suffer where
    We mock and hurt. Now he forgives
    Us for all that. For that he lives.

But though the heart of mystery
    Is his own right, he understands
Our simple hearts. In history
    He comes with little helpless hands
    But all who choose will be saved by
Means of a child who has to lie

Shivering, he clings fast to
    A virgin's breast, finds comfort there.
All stars are his, all wisdom too
    But for our sake he comes down here
    And we wait for his little hand
That all the world may understand.

Makings

Early we start making
Worlds and empires, even a language, often
At least a civil war.

Is war then in the blood
Early on? I still believe in a Fall,
That crucial one that made us feel ashamed,
Afraid of our bodies, putting out our hands
In the many crevices. We were frightened too
But of what? Afraid of being afraid and so
Building intimate castle walls, deep moats,
Guards night and day on duty?

One of the worlds I made with a friend of mine
Needed a totem pole with figures on it
(My friend was clever with paint brushes)
We made alarms and many mild tortures too.
Our world had a singular God
Who lived round every cloud but sometimes showed
Part of his face to us.
He had a cunning smile.
So we made ourselves new fears, new treasures too.
Explanations were not
Needed, 'Here' and 'Is' and 'When' and Now'
Were spectacular words indeed for things we only
Occasionally glimpsed. And of course we shaped a language,
Tiny Pentecosts of fiery sounds,
Whistles, shouting, whispers on the edge
Of understanding something. To ask was all,
To build a grammar, send up vast balloons
And wings and feathers and hushes and trembling forms.

This world endured throughout a Summer and
We were rulers, lawyers, singers, fliers
And finally we blew our world away
In rage and purpose and want and touching wood
And then came the words we did not want to say –
The end of a holiday.

Two Sonnets on Words and Music

I

Music leaps the language of our verse,
The sonnet does not have its brass or strings,
Percussion echoes with a sweet excess
And violins say more than lingerings

Of language. Poetry has to fight our tongue
And keep it pure and hold a message too.
The double-bass is neither old nor young
Yet carries meanings which we listen to.

The angel on a cloud will always hold
A lute or trumpet. Music is its sphere.
Poetry must be cautious, music's bold

And yet, and yet a great ode takes us where
The mystic looks to language to unfold
And cries out for the mastery of prayer.

II

Then there is Bach and counterpoint where meaning
Has no purpose. People always have
Set words to music from mankind's beginning,
And specially when all the drift is love.

But what of silence? Language uses there
Length or briefness till a verse is won.
And that's a chance or gift. Gift I prefer.
Love of man or God has always run

To words and cadence. Feelings must be said
And in as new a way as we can find.
The lover may not take an ode to bed

But knows right love occupies the mind
And by it he is willing to be led,
And by its brilliance only is struck blind.

Mid-May Meditation

How can I find a music of the heart
That marries mind and the imagination?
     I need the painter's brush and canvas and
Each composer's personal pattern which
     Engages us but also takes us further
Into the arms of dear discoveries.
     Today is burning May, I've drawn the curtains.
Since flooding, icy Winter we have been
     Through every climate in the calendar.
Many have lost a home which surely is
     A kind of death the spirit must accept.

     I'm in a mood of gratitude for so
Much richness in my life, enduring friends,
     An art to practise and a zest that is
A leaping passion. Mid-May is a blessing
     For students at work, in love or out of it.
I praise the vernal leaves, the seeking rainbows,
     The flowers around and hanging in their baskets.
I want a music of pure thankfulness,
     Horns and trumpets and the cellos too.
Saying 'Thank you' is inadequate,
     I need the sounds that satisfy like prayer.

Small Hours

The small hours are so big for me
And I can feel the stars draw near
In more than mere astronomy.
They are great lives I need not fear,
     No astrology

Is needed by me, I feel faith
In such wise being, life and power.
Time has no purpose. I'm graced with
A solitude that seems to flower
     Into a company

Of light, more light. O it is sweet
Simply to be. All wisdoms come
And make a kind and gentle home.
Stars are a bright simplicity
They write these words, make poems complete.

Myths Within Us

All the great myths that were whispered
    Into our childhood ears
Stay with us somehow somewhere
    Coming to life in tears

Or in great bursts of laughter,
    Jokes which went on while the sun
Was slowly, precisely going
    Leaving so much undone.

But the favours of Midas or Ajax,
    The Trojans' triumph, the old
Norse legends are written inside us
    And only will grow cold

When what we call our spirits
    Finally disappear
Yet most of us still believe even death
    Will keep those great gods near.

Song of Welcome

How swiftly and sweetly
        The weather can change
As if for your coming
        My power could arrange

The bold sun's appearance,
        The rain gone for good,
The whole world is wearing
        Its best clothes. The mood

In my heart is all glowing,
        No cloud is in sight,
The blue air is growing.
        There'll be no night, tonight.

I'll lay out a carpet
        Not red but all gold,
I've fashioned a wonder,
        An unfallen world.

A Metaphysical Point About Poetry

You said we only share what intellect
Provides us with. I can't agree with you.
Surely we share our love. We give it to
Express right feeling. Why, then, can't an act

Be shared? It manifestly is. Of course
You spoke of poetry and how it's true,
It is a making and so poets do
In little what God does with all his force

And all the time. I wish to say that God
Is present in all poetry that's made
With form and purpose. Everything that's said
Is written to be said. When poems are good

We say that they communicate. It's true
And surely like all truth it can be shared.
Tell me if my judgement is impaired
And why my poems can't share. I want them to.

Pain

Innocence is broken every day,
Shattered, wounded sometimes in the name
Of education, mostly in the way
Elders wreak some vengeance and then claim
      An innocent to say

Or, much more likely, show, for they lack words.
Think of the first time you found love and were
Enthralled. Some soldiers came with unsheathed swords
      And taught you how to fear.

So many ways to hate, yet more to love
And one man cried out from a cross to men
Who'd heard him say that he was God, with rough
Anger of their own nailed him in pain.
      On Calvary, no love

However twisted or perverse was not
Called upon for help. Obsequious men
Of law and church explained they had not thought
That God could bleed and weep, be all of pain
      And cry, know anguish yet.

Prayer for Holy Week

Love me in my willingness to suffer
Love me in the gifts I wish to offer
    Teach me how you love and have to die
      And I will try

Somehow to forget myself and give
Life and joy so dead things start to live.
    Let me show now an untrammelled joy,
      Gold without alloy.

You know I have no cross but want to learn,
How to change and to the poor world turn.
    I can almost worship stars and moon
      And the sun at noon

But when I'm low I only beg you to
Ask me anything, I'll try to do
    What you need. I trust your energy.
      Share it then with me.

Love's Struggle

Always this struggle of the flesh with mind,
The touch-and-go, the desperate waywardness,
Duality is dominant, we find
And never keeps the whole of happiness,

But we go on pursuing and retreating,
Now in a noble effort, now in low
Surrender. There is never perfect meeting
And, at the best, we quickly rise and grow

Away from one another but we come
Back to a sweet composure that can't last
Although we trust it can. We seem at home

But only for a moment. Time will cast
All sweets aside and we are blind and dumb,
Wanting forevers, finding only past.

'Hours' and Words

There is a sense of sunlight where
Warm messages and eager words
Are sent across the turning air,
Matins, little Hours and Lauds,

When people talk and hope to teach
A happiness that they have found.
Here prayer finds a soil that's rich
And sets a singing underground.

Let there be silence that is full
Of blossoming hints. When it is dark
Men's minds can link and their words fill
A saving boat that is God's ark.

O language is a precious thing
And ministers deep needs. It will
Soothe the mind and softly sing
And echo forth when we are still.

Song

I ought to know after so long
Trying to learn the art of verse
That it's large passion makes the song.
Long practice tells me love demurs

And waits in hiding till the art
Of singing, making build one whole.
Thus we can tell what breaks the heart
And lends compassion to the soul.

Craftsmen

I love to see the master at his work,
Concentrated wholly on his craft,
Whatever flaw may show, he will not shirk
To mend it, and whatever may be left

That's wasteful will be used for something else.
I think of carpenters and painters who
Build a house that never will seem false
Because it's painted, mended and made true

By sleight of hand and eye, and by the skill
That is particular and not to be
Copied by anyone. Man's choosing will

Loves the precise and measured, longs to see
The perfect box or bridge or waterwheel
And never needs to sign what he's set free.

For Seamus Heaney

I love you for the feel of things you have,
The nub, the texture, rub and block and blow.
I love the way you tell the touch, the heave,
The roll, the plait, the smooth, the working glow.

Nothing is alien that is of the earth,
And sky and water too. You are a kind
Of Adam who can bring all things to birth
And give emotion empire over mind.

You're not like Yeats. His Irishness was why
Causes are just and golden cities built.
He could polish jewels and paint the sky
But you care how a child, a bird has felt.

You hoard but often let us look at things
Like an old, rubbed satchel or the bite
Of saw on wood. You've made your children swings,
Cherished old cribs, made a newspaper kite.

Yes, maybe that is it; the rush and sheer
Marvel of air goes riding by your power.
What's used and tough is always to you dear.
The hedgerow for you, never one picked flower.

'The music of what happens' are your words
And happenings, not craft too judged are yours.
You find much pleasure watching playing-cards,
And you're all male yet not ashamed of tears.

The Book of Love

I have been reading in the book of love
　　　With all its exploits and
Withdrawals and advances. There's much of
　　　How we misunderstand
The ways of love. I have just turned a leaf
　　　And read about the end

Of falling into love and living it.
　　　I marvel as I turn
The pages. We can love with eyes and wit,
　　　There is so much to learn.
Love, though felt otherwise, is what we earn
　　　Although no price is set.

The sweets of it, of course, can't be kept long.
　　　We are not made for such.
Love that poets re-fashion in a song
　　　Is sometimes what we touch
But we cannot maintain this, love lasts long
　　　If we don't question much.

Who, knowing all the pain of love that breaks,
　　　Would not swear all was worth
The anger and remorse? True loving makes
　　　Allowances. Our earth
Can make the crudest gesture lively with
　　　Kind purpose which awakes.

The very comets which we watched last night
Yield us small visions of enduring light.

In a Bar

Who knows what he is feeling, this one here
Close to me in space but both of us
Might be two planets, each in different air?
I'm waiting to meet friends, have time to pass.

He tries to hide his eyes. What is his need?
He may, of course, be happy. Nonetheless
He's doing nothing, has no book to read.
Before him stands one small, long-empty glass.

Where will he be at midnight? Quite alone
Or in the arms of some girl he adores?
We are a foot apart, both on our own.

How poignant flesh and bone are just because
In love's act we can be a moment one
And then once more relearning all of loss.

The First Time

Our love is not the same as others'. We
Resent comparison for there was no love
Before we met. This makes us whole and free.
None has moved before the way we move

And never will. Our letters speak of things
New to the world. All's a discovery
For us. We find a new place and it sings
Up to the stars with our own melody.

Must we wait until love's lived with and
Domesticated, to find out we're wrong?
Or is it worse when we don't understand

Each others moods and thoughts, when every song
Dies with its echo? Now we're hand in hand
Within our world where others don't belong.

The Limits of Love

I

'I know what you feel,' we glibly say
And then continue 'I know what you think,'
And we speak of ourselves. We should obey
The courtesy of things. Through one small chink

Or key-hole we may glimpse a little of
Another's suffering but that is all.
Even when we murmur, 'O I love
You' our words are really but a personal call.

In truth we are surprised at likenesses
And say with honesty, 'Just now I thought
Something of what you mean,' and then we bless

Each other for a moment when we've caught
The other's spirit and large purposes.
We live by guesswork and the time is short

II

When we felt we were one. But then, of course,
In love we scarcely need a word at all
Since by a touch, a gaze, we learn the force
Of passion and repose. When people fall

Asleep when they have loved, they cannot share
A dream. We have to learn a desolation.
There is no art to show us how to bear
Closeness in sleep. We fall away from passion

And we don't know that sleep may take us to
All the unknown places of the heart.
In consciousness at least, we know man's true

Loneliness. But when we have to start
Sleeping no map tells us where to go.
We enter lands of which we know no part.

After an Elegy
(for my sister)

Now you're learning all of loneliness
Which is quite different from solitude.
Feeling lonely is complete distress
But being solitary is a mood

A poet, for example, needs to write,
A wise man wants for thinking out the world;
Loneliness, you'll find, is almost cold,
You linger near the sun and beg its light.

Your husband's dead and you have lived all through
The anger and the shock. This week now you
Gain another grandchild. You can go
Through all life's starting phases, see the new

With joy and pure delight. A child, you were
A little mother often, would push me
About when I had fallen. Birth is near
Now but death dogs you. You have to see

The empty pillow and your house so still.
I wish that I could teach you how to be
Happy by yourself but, falteringly,
You must live on with your own steadfast will.

Let me offer you imagination,
An opulence of stories about love,
I know that round your house in isolation
You walk. True grief like yours will not move off

Swiftly but you have new life at hand,
A little girl to hold within your arms
And she will need you. Being needed calms
As you so long ago could understand.

A Gift of Gratitude
(for Christina)

This house is Number Thirteen and is full
      Of wisdom and of love.
The four girls who grew up here cast a spell
And in their home you feel a spirit move

And it is kind. O yes, there has been pain.
      The mother of these girls
Can sail and ski but has also lived in
Self-doubt and all the bitterness that fills

The tension of divorce. She has not let
      It make her sour. She is
Full of natural wisdom and has set
Her children free in her own happiness.

When trouble stormed me she gave me a home.
      Three months she offered me
And laid upon me all the gifts that come
To the right sufferers. She would be

Light-hearted, dazzling, also calm and free,
      A freedom she's worked for.
I want to write a lively poem, to say
I've learnt so much, so deftly too from her.

Praise can sound sentimental, gratitude
      Twists our English speech.
Let me offer then a spell-like mood
Which few can learn and fewer still can teach.

At Our Best

There are so many loves we know,
Paternal kind, and one we feel
For somebody who's understood
Or nursed us when we're weak. We go
About in search of one which seemed
To find us at our best always,
The best of love won't fill our days.

It is ample and we have
A mind and heart not deep or wide
Enough for such a love to fill.
For this Christ cried out from a hill
Hoping God's love in him as man
Would find us ready. Sloth or pride
Found us wanting. I've a plan,

One that found me, gave me rest
And love beyond our frail desires,
Compassion thriving at its best.
Even when we're found wanting, Christ
Let's us choose again. The Tree
Of Paradise turned to the one

Where God as man cried out for us
To show us joyfully that need
He begged for. We did not refuse
For he was taken from the Cross
Where Mary and his great friend stood,
Our representatives. And thus
All mankind in time and out
Forgets the selfishness of doubt
And finds it easy to be good.

The Largest Question

I've vexed my mind about where spirits are
And how they manage when death's taken off
Their pelt of flesh through which the senses stir
And act and do our will, at best
Beyond the flesh and more.

And yet when love's the drift we gladly work
Through every sense we have and shape a world
Where marvels happen and where we can mark
With flesh, and where we feel our spirit bold
Until we reach the dark.

The dark of absences and loss by death
We hide and long to have our dearest back
But life and death are always but a breath
Apart. What happens when the largest lack
Parts us from this world with

Slowness or suddenness? And what and where
Does God, we say we trust, move all of us?
My greatest friend was good and she is where
The spirit's lively. O but she is loss
And I am lost to her.

Does she know moonlight and the ocean's wash
Around this planet? Does she now at last
Learn perfectly the love she knew as flesh?
Her glowing spirit surely can't be past
And so each day I wish

That she were present with her liveliness,
Enchantment too which she would press on me.
She often was the whole of happiness.
O God, instruct me where she now must be
Without the cruel sickness

That was a dreadful death-in-life for her.
She was imperial and became a slave,
She was indomitable, kept all fear
Away from me. O God, she still is dear
In every curling wave,

In every cooling wind, her mind was brimmed
With precious knowledge which she gave away
And still more came. Such life cannot be dimmed.
Her spirit moves in all good words I say
And surely part of me

Is in little what her great soul knows.
She is with God who must delight in her
And set her still a-dance. I think she goes
Where God keeps spirits out of time before
Life is all rise, not rose.

Concerning History

I

Does history guess itself into our minds,
    Taking over our memories, railing at our past,
        Envious of our future?

Let there be a lullaby for all
    Events that history cannot avoid.
        It listens to prayers, it comforts youth,
        It mocks the aged.

Listen, history is now and what you're doing,
    It is the seed that grew, it is the child
        In a green wood in a gold flower in a white hour.
        Don't let grey come banging the door.
        It's the ghost of a ghost
        It's not history's death.
        It is hope distracted,
        Passion dissected.

Does history tell love-stories?
    That's not its one aim
        But Cleopatra makes Antony include themselves,
        Eloise again breaks the will of Abelard.

History also lies down in the fields
    And picks the berries in an eclogue day.
        History is not divided though it sometimes seems so.
        Too often it's broken pieces of wise men and
        wars of foolish ones.

History's a game
    But you have to play it seriously,
        Not let your mind be distracted,
        Speak only the slang of the game.
        Quiet, quiet. Does history really sleep?
        I have lost it, I have lost it and
        I weep.

*

History must deal with us and
          you and you.
          and we and me and all those behind
          who fit their lively shadows
          whose deaths were marked by war
          whose purposes were order and design
          who loved the new-made and the new-born too.

History is so tangled, is also
so guessing forward;
it is urgent, tragic.
We are part of it for its
concerns are wide and forward and old and new,
it uses mirrors and magnifying glasses,
it argues with the geography of time
and won't leave meteorology alone.

History is also tender,
more than benign.
It is intimate,
it enters all our dreams but
won't abuse
the humble lives we are,

And in the end and always
the great historian selects a line.
Deep in encyclopaedias he is
but also must give many years and much endeavour.

History selects the credos of the world.
          The first wild
                    rustic gods,
The proud large spirits of sophistication.
To write your history is a daring thing
and also it requires much ruthlessness.

O yes yes yes yes yes yes
but it is gentle, childlike, lyrical.
History makes an orchestra of time,
and all the instruments men have designed
will bow before the lovely human voice.
The order of a king,

the servants' obligations
and will are at the heart of this austere
and yet also at times this golden study.

*

The reverie, the dream,
     The quick word and the long
Sound of coming home
     And then the sleeping song,
The haunting of the flesh,
     The unripe touch upon
Another's world. The wish
     that cannot be undone.
This is a little of all history's music.
     Its war-cries, its peace treaties
     and always, always its search for some design.
Not one imposed but one lived out in time
from the huge epic to the nursery rhyme.

*

Pacts and treaties
     Heresies and arguments.
        The guess that grows,
           The malice that moves
             In so many places

But most in the human heart:
     History lodges there a little,
        It must remember the unguarded hour,

Balance and value
     Weighing up
        Looking down
           At all of us over the globe,
             Smaller than ants when we are dust
               But quick with kind dreams and
                  gold wishes

                    Moving up and down
                              Over and into
                              And leaping and dancing
                    With a scholar's meditation.

The great historian is always listening.
His countless notebooks
          His findings and guesses
          Wait for months, for years
          Till only wisdom moves his daring hopes,
Only self-sacrifice gives him truths to give us
          part of our story.
We are the punctuation-marks he must use precisely
          in his lucid style.

II

From legends and myths
From scarab and stone
From yellowing rolls
Bills and receipts
Faded papyrus
Tomb-stones
Tall stories – take on any or all, these are the base
The starting and stopping
Often going back beyond Greece or Rome
Checking, balancing
Putting together
Almost unbearable
Difficult hours
When the facts won't fit or are not facts.

Turn to the fax,
The computer, the ruler,
the filing cabinet,
every modern convenience
put to the service of knowledge.

All to be placed together,
          so many notes to discard,
          too many contradictions,
          too many false roads taken.

The historian moves from his study,
walks into the garden
and sees a grandchild making a daisy-chain.

'That's my purpose,' he thinks,
watching the adequate fingers,
loving the whole picture
when the facts won't fit
or are not facts,

'And what then of love?' he observes,
'It rides and wishes and is joyful
Over the story of man.
The king hated his mistress
That politician was impotent.
Should I be reading more novels?
O mankind you slip from my hand
But I can do nothing without you.'

III

Theories of history –
Get the facts right and a pattern emerges.
Watch the clock, the clothes,
The political choices
And time slips into its place.

How to address the spirit?
No use to list creeds and cults, no help
To file or correlate,
To give mere likenesses.
History itself has a spirit,
It shows in the movements of men
at their extreme moments,
when they are most hopeful
and when they are daunted by death, the sufferings
of others and their own.

What then of God?
In every stage of man and all his making
He has been a creator.
Even in unbelief he's pursued the good.

60

History has no trouble with the wicked.
Recording it may be a tenth of its purpose
    And all the choices of action.
History is words.
Visions are not always spoken or written
But history is in the spine of mankind's book,
His book is belief in God,
Be quiet and listen, listen;
There are whispers outside my window,
It is July but wet and cool as April,
Seasons work on and through history.

Tomorrow is Sunday and many
Visit a church
Pray to a God
Beg forgiveness
Tonight is the end of the Sabbath
The Synagogues are shut.

History whispers in the waiting ear
And hints how power may be obtained, how war
Has to occur. Dictators see themselves
As near-gods worthy of their people's love
And what is more they take that love for granted.
Often their armies march through frontiers,
Soldiers are helpers, make men orderly,
But the despot argues and for long
His words have been believed. 'He is good,'
The people say and offer laurel leaves,
But history throws them off, is on the move

    Chasing
        chasing
            chasing
                all of us.
It sets a rainbow over millions dead
    and someone somewhere
        counts again the colours,
Tributes to who we are and
    all our story . . .